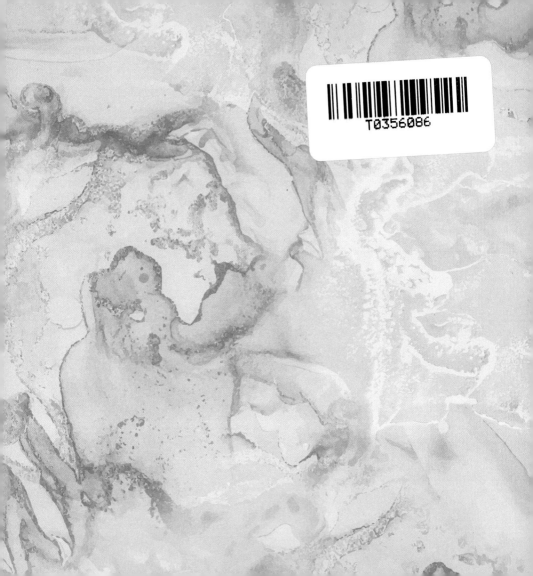

THANK YOU

Mom

Keepsake Gift Book

A Gift For:

_____

From:

_____

Thank you for providing strength
and encouragement every day.
Thank you for being my rock.

For teaching me that it's not about what you have, but how you patch it all together that makes a beautiful life.

"When you are looking at your mother, you are looking at the purest love you will ever know."

—Charley Benetto

Thank you for making every day brighter, even when it rains.

For convincing me that my art could hang in any museum in the world, but the refrigerator door was the grandest place of all!

"Mothers are like glue. Even when you can't see them, they're still holding the family together."

—Susan Gale

Thank you for being the strength
that holds our family through
the good and the bad.

For showing that love is the center
of the greatest gift of all—family.

"A mother is your first friend, your best friend, your forever friend."

—Amit Kalantri

Thank you for being the seam
that stitches our family together.

For being my biggest fan, cheering me on no matter what.

"My mother was my role model before
I even knew what that word was."

—Lisa Leslie

Thank you for your hugs that make everything better.

For teaching me that even
the smallest things in life are
often the most beautiful.

"Life began with waking up
and loving my mother's face."

—George Eliot

Thank you for making me
the person I am today.

For showing me how to overcome
life's unexpected obstacles.

"Successful mothers are not the ones who have never struggled. They are the ones who never gave up despite the struggles."

—Sharon Jaynes

Thank you for your patience during those times when I didn't follow your advice and had to learn on my own.

For unraveling my worries with
your comforting words.

"Mothers hold their children's hands for a short while, but their hearts forever."

—Nitya Prakash

Thank you for teaching me that first steps are always hard.

For quilting a legacy of love
that will last for generations.

"If love is as sweet as a flower, then my mother is that sweet flower of love."

—Stevie Wonder

Thank you for teaching me
when to hold on tight and when
it's time to let something go.

For your laughter, which always
fills the room with joy.

"My mother is my root, my foundation. She planted the seed that I base my life on, and that is the belief that the ability to achieve starts in your mind."

—Michael Jordan

Thank you for celebrating my successes and supporting me no matter how hard I fumble.

For your endless love.

"Mothers are the people who love us for no good reason. And those of us who are mothers know it's the most exquisite love of all."

—Maggie Gallagher

Thank you for being
my MOM!

Images from Shutterstock.com: luciann.photography (3); Stanislav Samoylik (5); Gina Hsu (7); Mircea
Costina (9); Pics Garden (11); Adventurer Marketing (13); Ivan Chistyakov (15); sun ok (17); Igor Poluchin (19);
mark higgins (21); MacBen (23); Usman Priyona (25); Carl V Boley (27); xxposure (29); A-photography (31);
Crisss12000 (33); JTTucker (35); Guy's Art (37); Volodymyr Yakovyna (39); Isabelle OHara (41); Triff (43); Eric
Isselee (45); Michael Warwick (47); Andrew Tuttle (49); Sergei Sokolnikov (51); happykamill (53); Denis Tabler
(55); mark higgins (57); Shavlovskiy (59); Michael Warwick (61); Stacey Newman (63).

ISBN 978-1-4971-0558-4

Library of Congress Control Number: 2024925890

To learn more about the other great books from Fox Chapel Publishing, or to find a retailer near you,
call toll-free 800-457-9112, or visit us at www.FoxChapelPublishing.com.

You can also send mail to:
903 Square Street
Mount Joy, PA 17552.

We are always looking for talented authors. To submit an idea, please send a brief inquiry to
acquisitions@foxchapelpublishing.com.

Printed in China

First printing